5 SECONDS OF SUMMER

CONFIDENTIAL

UNOFFICIAL AND UNAUTHORIZED

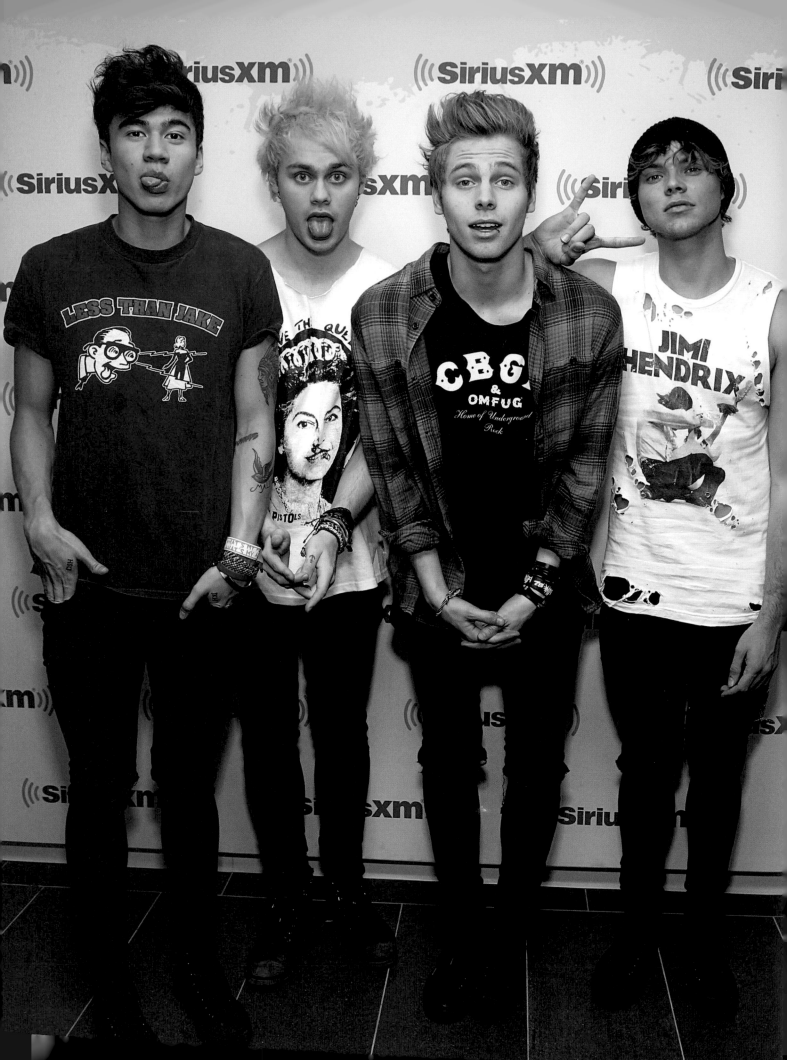

5 SECONDS OF SUMMER

CONFIDENTIAL

UNOFFICIAL AND UNAUTHORIZED

OVER 100 AMAZING PHOTOGRAPHS OF THE WORLD'S HOTTEST BOY BAND

PRESTON BESLEY

CARLTON BOOKS

MICHAEL

LUKE

ASHTON

CALUM

CONTENTS

Hard work, dedication, and great fans have taken 5SOS to the very top.

5SOS has earned a reputation for their electrifying, high-energy live performances.

THE RISE AND RISE OF FIVE SECONDS OF SUMMER

5 Seconds of Summer—Five-Ess-Oh-Ess, Five SOS, or Five Sauce, as their fans call them—are four feisty Australian musicians who have taken the world by storm. Their rise from Sydney schoolboys to pop phenomenon has been meteoric. Fueled by fabulous punk-pop songs, a colossal social media profile, and an ever-growing army of devoted fans, their fantastic journey is far from over.

Their first single, "She Looks So Perfect," reached the top spot in a staggering 39 countries in just two days, and their debut album, released in August 2014, went to No. 1 in the U.S., the U.K., and 69 other countries. Their own headlined shows now sell out in minutes, screaming fans mob them at airports, and millions follow them on Twitter. But stardom hasn't changed Luke (guitar and vocals), Michael (guitar), Calum (bass guitar and vocals), and Ashton (drums). They still love playing music, fooling around, and—most of all—meeting their fans.

5 Seconds of Summer Confidential is your chance to discover the band as never before. It tells the inside story of the laughs and adventures the guys have had along the way, and gives you the lowdown on each member of the band. And, of course, it's bursting with amazing photographs of Luke, Michael, Calum, and Ashton at work and at play.

COMING TOGETHER

FROM A SCHOOL MUSIC ROOM TO WORLDWIDE FAME, IT'S BEEN A WHIRLWIND JOURNEY FOR THE BOYS OF 5SOS.

America, here we come! 5SOS salute their fans after appearing on NBC's *The TODAY Show* in New York.

An unexciting suburb of Sydney is not the obvious place to give birth to the hottest new band on the planet. In sports-crazed Australia, few in their home city gave the boys a second glance. As Ashton says, "It's not a nurturing place for music."

However, in 2011 in a music room in Norwest Christian College, 30 miles (48 km) from the city center, something was stirring. Two fifteen-year-olds, Luke Hemmings and Michael Clifford, had finally put aside a long-held schoolboy animosity, realized they liked each other, and joined up with their mutual friend Calum Hood to play guitar and sing together. As Michael tells it, "We sort of gravitated towards each other 'cause we were like the outcasts at school. It just wasn't cool what we were doing."

What they were doing was playing songs they loved—songs like "Teenage Dirtbag" by Wheatus and Ed Sheeran's "The A Team." Luke uploaded the videos to Facebook and they suddenly discovered there were people out there who liked their sound. "We never tried to be anything we weren't," he explains. "We just put up stuff that was real

Michael at 15 (with his natural hair color!), rocking out in the school auditorium.

A 14-year-old Luke goes solo for Performance Night at Norwest Christian College in 2010.

and I think people like real people, and fans really respond when you respond to them."

The fledgling group needed a name. When all Luke could come up with was "Bromance," it was left to Michael to get his thinking cap on. "I wanted a name that people could add their own name to, like 5 Seconds of Calum," he remembers. He texted his genius idea—5 Seconds of Summer—to the other two. Neither was impressed. Still, somehow it stuck.

Their YouTube covers were now gathering hits, particularly an acoustic version of Chris Brown and Justin Bieber's "Next 2 You." Then, it was time for a gig. Calum offered to switch to bass guitar and Michael contacted a drummer friend of a friend through Facebook. "Do you wanna play a gig to like, 200 people?" he messaged Ashton.

In fact, only twelve people turned up for the first 5SOS live show at a downtown Sydney hotel

The hairstyles change, the clothes change, but these are those same Sydney boys.

PHILLY

"WE SORT OF GRAVITATED TOWARDS EACH OTHER 'CAUSE WE WERE LIKE THE OUTCASTS AT SCHOOL." Michael

Michael and Calum on stage together at Performance Night. Luke was watching his soon-to-be bandmates.

on December 3, 2011. It wasn't spectacular, but the boys loved the thrill of performing. As soon as the show ended, Calum got down on one knee to propose that their drummer join the band permanently. Recruiting him really drove the group forward. Ashton insisted they took it seriously, rehearsing six days a week, gigging more, and even writing their own songs.

Then it happened. "We were told Louis Tomlinson [of One Direction] had found us on YouTube," says Ash. "He really liked what we were doing. We were like, 'Woah!'" The One Direction singer had tweeted a link to the band's track "Gotta Get Out." The big time was calling. The boys left school—by that time, their minds hadn't been on their schoolbooks for quite a while. They got themselves a manager and, as their YouTube views rose to the hundreds of thousands, they started playing shows across Australia.

The four boys, still in their teens, said goodbye to their quiet Sydney suburb. They now had online fans in every continent and it was time to meet them.

5SOS
MAKING MUSIC

HOW A HARDWORKING LIVE BAND EARNED CHART-TOPPING ALBUM SUCCESS—WITH A LITTLE HELP FROM THEIR MUSICAL HEROES.

"THEY'RE ALL REALLY GOOD AT WHAT THEY DO. I WAS JUST BLOWN AWAY."

Jon Feldman, producer

The four guys who just wanted to rock out playing versions of their favorite songs have come a long way. "I remember the first band practice in Michael's garage," says Luke. "Calum didn't have a bass. There was one microphone we'd all share and Ashton was on an electric drum kit."

Success hasn't happened overnight. The boys put in long hours of practice, working and working at their songs until they developed into a great live band. They weren't content with just playing covers, though—they wanted to write their own songs. So, in 2012 they traveled to London to hone their song-writing talents.

A guitar and a voice —who needs lights and a stage to give a star performance?

Playing acoustic and electric sets enables the boys to rock out and play anywhere.

In the U.K. they teamed up with some of their all-time heroes, including Alex Gaskarth from All Time Low and the Madden brothers of Good Charlotte. The boys would divide up in pairs; usually Michael with Ashton and Calum with Luke, and each pair had a mentor. "Michael and Ashton are goofballs," says Alex Gaskarth. "They brought a ton of energy to the songs we wrote together." And the others? "Calum and Luke were kind of the quiet ones at first, [but] once we got going, they started to come out of their shells."

The guys brought their own ideas to the sessions. They wrote about what they knew— about girls and about feeling like social outcasts. "We like to write stories within songs," explains Luke. They worked on almost one hundred new songs before they finally felt ready to record. "We wanted to stay under the radar for as long as we could—now is the time for us to really show the world what we're about," said Ashton on the eve of the release of their debut EP *She Looks So Perfect*.

5SOS entered the recording studio ready to work hard at creating a great album. Their producer, Jon Feldman, commented, "They're all really good at what they do. I was just blown

5SOS has worked hard to create a pulsating live show that leaves their fans breathless.

Intimate shows at radio stations enable 5SOS to get close to their fans.

away." He describes how Luke's guitar parts give the songs an anthemic feel and how Michael comes into his own on the guitar solos in addition to chanting the choruses. When it came to their singing, he encouraged them to be themselves, to stick to their Australian accents. He says Calum has the "cleanest voice and best pitch," while Ashton is a natural when it comes to the harmonies.

5SOS the album, with all but one of the songs penned by the band, went straight to No. 1 on iTunes in 69 different countries on the day after its release—proof that the band that started out in a dingy garage had made it to the very top.

Luke steps up while Michael and Calum show off some of their moves while on stage.

"CALUM DIDN'T HAVE A BASS. THERE WAS ONE MICROPHONE WE'D ALL SHARE AND ASHTON WAS ON AN ELECTRIC DRUM KIT." Luke

PROFILE
LUKE

LUKE IS THE GROUP'S SCORCHING HOT FRONT MAN. BUT BEHIND THE GOOFING AROUND AND PUNK ATTITUDE LIES ONE HOME-LOVING MAMA'S BOY.

Luke in Las Vegas. Is he wondering what Mom is up to back in Australia?

Leaping for joy, Luke in action as 5SOS returns to Sydney in 2014.

Standing-tall, looking good, and a great guitarist—Luke makes the perfect front man.

Not long ago, Luke was living back in Riverstone, Australia, with his math teacher mom (she even taught Ashton for a year!) and rock music-loving Dad. Luke is the baby of the family and he used to "borrow" his big brothers' clothes and pick up the guitars they left lying around. In high school, Luke had long hair and drooping bangs and wore luminous green shades. The other kids—including his future bandmates—decided he was just too cool for school and left him alone. So, instead of hanging out at lunch, Luke headed for the music room to practice guitar. After hooking up with Michael and Calum, his lonely days were over. The band was taking shape.

The boys were soon the best of friends, traveling the world together. Luke's energy, cheerfulness, and crazy falsetto cries keep the gang sane while on the road. He always has a smile on his face, but he takes his job in the band seriously. Calum says, "He always chooses the sensible thing to do." The flip side? Well, they all agree—along with his mom—that Luke is a bad roommate. Ashton

Luke has a special bond with his fans and has appeared in thousands of selfies.

reveals, "Luke is a very messy shower-taker and frustrating to live with!" Michael adds, "He also steals underwear! ... He comes into our rooms and takes it when we're not there."

On stage, Luke is an awesome singer and a pretty mean guitarist. He builds a special relationship with his audience and it continues off stage—he's an obsessive tweeter (3 million followers) and Instagrammer (another 4 million). The more we find out about Luke, the more fun he seems—he's amazing at snapping his fingers in rhythm, his favorite underpants have pictures of SpongeBob SquarePants on them, and he

"LUKE ALSO STEALS UNDERWEAR! ... HE COMES INTO OUR ROOMS AND TAKES IT WHEN WE'RE NOT THERE." Michael

doesn't mind if his fans sneak into concerts without buying a ticket!

Although we see him messing around onstage, pulling pranks with the rest of the band and constantly joking in interviews, that doesn't stop him from missing his friends, family, and life back in Australia. His famous tweet, "And yes, I'm a mummy's boy..." confirmed what we all suspected,

Luke's rock star good looks make him a hit with 5SOS fans.

Luke in full stride during the Final of *The Voice of Italy* in June 2014.

"Hemmo" channels the punk spirit as 5SOS raises the tempo.

A pause for breath during their show-stopping performance for the MTV Video Music Awards.

"HE'S 7 FEET 5 INCHES TALL, HIS HAIR IS ALWAYS ERECT, HE'S 75% LEGS, HE'S READY FOR ANYTHING!" Michael

so he was overjoyed when his mom joined him in America for a few days. She wasn't impressed by his rock 'n' roll lifestyle, though. He tweeted, "The judgemental tone when you try order breakfast at 2!"

Luke has dreamy blue eyes, gravity-defying blond hair, a simply gorgeous smile, and a lip ring. All these, and his long, long legs, have made him a heartthrob. But Luke's been single ever since 5SOS hit the road, so his bandmates came up with a dating profile for him. It said, "He's 7 feet 5 inches tall, his hair is always erect, he's 75% legs, he's ready for anything!"

Luke definitely appreciates the band's fantastic female following, though, and maybe one day he might even date a fan. After all, he says, "It would be a bit awkward to be with a girlfriend who didn't love what you do!"

5SOS IN NORTH AMERICA

5SOS DREAMED OF PLAYING THEIR SONGS IN NORTH AMERICA. WHEN THEIR DREAM CAME TRUE, IT WAS WILDER AND MORE INCREDIBLE THAN THEY EVER IMAGINED.

5SOS completes their journey from a Sydney garage to the biggest stages in the world.

hen One Direction invited 5SOS to join their *Take Me Home Tour* in 2013, it was hard for the guys to contain their excitement. It was the break they'd dreamed of and a chance to perform in front of thousands. Michael, for one, was stunned. "It's amazing. When we started, I just assumed the U.S. was out of reach. When you start a band, you kind of just do it for fun. You can never expect what's going to happen... It's just amazing."

So 5SOS took to the stage for a three-month tour that spanned the U.S., as well as three dates in Canada. 5SOS was virtually unknown in the States, but with each event date that was changing fast. They played huge arenas, learning valuable lessons from 1D every night. "Just the way they handle day-to-day life being One Direction, it's a cool thing to watch," observed Ashton.

Within the year, 5SOS was back across the Atlantic, this time touring as headliners. Their fabulously named *Stars, Stripes, and Maple Syrup Tour* took in ten dates in venues across the U.S. and Canada. Although the band had officially released only a few songs, they were amazed that their fans sang along with every word. "They'd had to get all the lyrics off YouTube," explained Calum to a bemused TV presenter.

New York in April 2014: 5SOS has just delivered another exhilarating show.

5SOS holding nothing back for the MTV Video Music Awards... And this was just the rehearsal!

Fun, excitement, intensity... the 5SOS live experience summed up in one photo.

"WHEN WE STARTED, I JUST ASSUMED THE U.S. WAS OUT OF REACH. WHEN YOU START A BAND, YOU KIND OF JUST DO IT FOR FUN." Michael

Goofing around backstage at the MGM
Grand Garden Arena in Las Vegas.

Calum owns the stage and an appreciative crowd signal their approval.

The tour was sensational. Their fans brought central New York to a standstill and created chaos at LAX airport in Los Angeles. Their setlist began with a rousing "18," which got the crowd on their feet and kept them there with favorites like "Amnesia" and "Beside You." Crowds loved the cover of Katy Perry's "Teenage Dream" and were in ecstasy by the time they finished up with the double whammy of their most popular songs "Good Girls" and "She Looks So Perfect."

Their debut album entered the U.S. *Billboard* chart at No. 1, selling more than a quarter of a million copies in the first week. It was the biggest splash made by a first album for nearly a decade. Even though their tour sold out in just five minutes, the band was astounded.

"THEY'D HAD TO GET ALL THE LYRICS OFF YouTube." Calum

No signs of nerves as the band gets ready to play to millions on U.S. television.

The boys answering questions on their now legendary appearance on NBC's *The TODAY Show*.

"It's more than any artist and band could expect," said Michael.

When they came back again with One Direction's *Where We Are Tour* in the fall of 2014, they visited massive stadiums with over 50,000 sold-out capacities. As Ashton told *Billboard* magazine, "It's good fun to work on your stage presence. It's a massive experience to actually be in a band and learn how to control a stadium." The guys took particular pride in inspiring a stadium full of American "boy band" fans to sing along to head-banging hit "Highway to Hell" by 80s Australian rockers AC/DC.

When the weary band of brothers finally left LA to go home to Sydney, they knew they had won over America. They had already planned their 2015 return with their *Rock Out With Your Socks Out Tour*. As Luke says, "I love America. It's a great place for our band."

GOT THE T-SHIRT!

WANT TO DISCOVER WHICH OTHER BANDS THE 5SOS GUYS LOOK UP TO? IT'S NOT DIFFICULT. JUST TAKE A LOOK AT THEIR T-SHIRTS.

There's usually a 5SOS member sporting a Nirvana shirt. This time it's Calum's turn.

These boys might wear their hearts on their sleeves, but they also wear their heroes on their chests. Flip through the photographs of them on and off stage, and you'll find an A to Z of rock T-shirts. For the boys, this is not just fashion, these are statements about music. Their T-shirts send the message, "This is our heritage. These are the bands we aim to emulate."

Their biggest influence? Undoubtedly it's the American Grammy-winning group Green Day. The Californian punk popsters had massive worldwide hits in the 90s and 2000s. Their singles "American Idiot" and "Boulevard of Broken Dreams" were the soundtrack to the lives of the 5SOS boys when they were just seven or eight years old.

Green Day shares a mixture of energy, spirit, and great sing-along tunes with bands like All Time Low and Blink 182, which grabbed the Sydney youngsters' attention. "We all were brought up in the time of Green Day and everything like that," confirms Ashton. "That type of music has just influenced us so much today."

The chorus of 5SOS's "End Up Here" opens with the lines, "How did we end up talking in the first place? You said you liked my Cobain shirt." When asked to name their all-time musical hero, three of the guys invariably reply "Kurt Cobain," the sadly departed singer of legendary grunge band Nirvana. Ash is the exception. He usually picks Nirvana's drummer, Dave Grohl. "You can tell our fans from a mile away," the boys once said. "They're the ones wearing Nirvana shirts."

Original punk rockers like the Sex Pistols, the Clash, and the Ramones also get the T-shirt seal of approval. The boys have worn emblems of all these famous bands because they admire their attitude and style—especially Michael, whose multicolored hairstyles come straight from the punk scene. "We're so proud of the music we make—we love it—and we're fearless," they have said. "If anyone puts us down, we don't care. Isn't that somewhat punk? Not giving a damn what people say?"

Australia doesn't have a massive musical heritage for the boys to shout about, but there is one Aussie band they will never let us forget. Hard rockers AC/DC are the only other Australian band that has made it to the top of the U.S. album charts. In a concert in Melbourne, Australia 5SOS even played a

Defiant pose and a classic rock guitar—all set off by a fabulous, iconic T-shirt.

cover of the band's megahit "Highway to Hell" after Ashton spotted his father in the audience wearing an AC/DC T-shirt.

The guys love to sport classic rock icons, too. The Rolling Stones, Queen, Jimi Hendrix, Pink Floyd, and Metallica have all graced the front of their T-shirts. The logos of modern groups like the Strokes, Paramore, and Canadian rockers Nickelback also feature in the boys' wardrobe. This all adds up to a huge pool of the heroes 5SOS look to as they create their own sound and style. "We're kind of like a big lovechild of all our influences," explains Michael. "We take pop influences to stay modern because ultimately we wanna modernize 90s and early-2000s rock with nowadays pop."

"WE ALL WERE BROUGHT UP IN THE TIME OF GREEN DAY AND EVERYTHING LIKE THAT. THAT TYPE OF MUSIC HAS JUST INFLUENCED US SO MUCH TODAY." Ashton

Ashton in an Anti-Nowhere League shirt. The drummer often shows his allegiance to lesser-known 1970s punk bands.

Ash tries to pretend he didn't get the "wear your best T-shirt" e-mail.

Mikey decides his Ozzy
shirt is so good it deserves
to be worn onstage.

ASHTON

ASH MIGHT HAVE BEEN LATE JOINING THE BAND, BUT HE'S MADE UP FOR IT WITH ENTHUSIASM, DRIVE, AND SHEER COMMITMENT TO THE 5SOS CAUSE.

Bandana, sleeveless T-shirt, and a big, big smile—that's the Ashton Irwin look.

With eyes that light up a room, the personal style of a real rock star, and an infectious sense of humor, Ashton looks every inch a 5SOS dude. It's hard to believe the group ever existed without him, yet the other three had known each other for years when Ash got the call. The band had arranged their first live gig and had no drummer. Did Ash want to play with them? "I met the other boys through mutual friends," he recalls. "They needed a drummer and that's where I came from. We played a gig at a really dingy, gross pub." Like the missing piece of a jigsaw, he clicked into place.

A year or more older than the rest of the boys, Ash was taught to play drums by his stepfather. He had already been in a band called Swallow the Goldfish, and now he had left school and was working in a video

"Ashton is just a natural when it comes to the harmonies," says their producer Jon Feldman.

"IF SOMEONE IN THE BAND HAS NO PANTS ON, YOU *ALL* MUST HAVE NO PANTS ON. BAND LAW!" Ashton

store when the call came. He didn't need to be asked twice. Ever since then, he has been the heart and soul of the group, a point hammered home by the 5SOS logo tattoo he proudly sports.

On stage, it is Ashton's pounding beat that powers the band forward. Off stage, it is his bubbly personality. In interviews, it is Ash who usually takes the lead. This might be because he's naturally chatty, or because he's the oldest band member. The rest of the boys certainly agree that Ash is like an older brother to them and the driving force behind the band. When he was hospitalized with appendicitis in October 2014, the boys' heartfelt wishes made it clear just how important Ash is to the group.

With boundless energy and enthusiasm, Ashton keeps the beat in another triumphant live show.

"I WANT THE AUDIENCE TO LEAVE FEELING LIKE THEY RAN A MARATHON. I WANT IT TO BE LOUD AND ROCK AND HIGH ENERGY." Ashton

In their live shows, Ash's commitment to the cause is obvious. He says he is so completely dripping with sweat after a concert that no one will come near him for an hour. "I want the audience to leave feeling like they ran a marathon," he says, explaining why he works so hard. "I want it to be loud and rock and high energy. I want it to be fun and capture the humor of the band at the same time."

He sounds just as much fun on the road. "I absolutely love being on a tour bus," he says. "It's kinda like a little time capsule. You go to sleep and wake up in another incredible place."

Ash is loving every minute of the band's amazing journey to the top.

"THEY NEEDED A DRUMMER AND THAT'S WHERE I CAME FROM. WE PLAYED A GIG AT A REALLY DINGY, GROSS PUB." Ashton

We've learned that he loves spaghetti, bandanas, and vanilla-scented candles, and that he likes girls who sport a rock-chick look. He is afraid of the dark and—according to the others—has the loudest snore on the bus. Ash is also responsible for the "no pants rule." In a slightly strange display of solidarity and brotherly love, he insists that, "If someone in the band has no pants on, you *all* must have no pants on. Band law!"

Most of all, Ash is proud of what the band has achieved. "It's been crazy," he says. "For people to actually care about the music and that stuff is incredible. It's a cool thing and we're very lucky and blessed."

He may have been the last in the band, but we couldn't imagine the boys without Ash now.

Ashton always has a gorgeous smile and a wave for his fabulous fans.

Ash gets competitive. "Hey, Mikey, I can stick my tongue out, too—look!"

HAVING FUN, ACTING CRAZY

FOR ONE OF THE HARDEST WORKING BANDS AROUND, 5SOS SURE MANAGE TO HAVE SOME FUN ON THEIR WAY AROUND THE WORLD.

Work hard, play hard. That seems to be the motto that Michael, Cal, Ash, and Luke live by. When they are not playing gigs, writing, or recording, there is usually some kind of craziness or mischief going on. Whether it's Michael's hilarious live feeds of his video gaming (he has a thing for *League of Legends*), an "ugly selfie" competition, or their splashing swimming pool antics, it's always party central with the boys—and always posted for their fans to see.

Given half a chance, the boys love to dress up. Who can forget the fun they had in their Teenage Mutant Ninja Turtle outfits when recording the video for "Don't Stop"? The turtles became a 5SOS obsession. Luke knew exactly who would play which turtle: Ashton had to be Donatello, Calum was Raphael, Michael was Michelangelo (of course), and he chose Leonardo. Then, on the last night of the 1D *Where We Are Tour*, they shocked the Miami crowd by rocking onstage in their turtle outfits.

On a day off in LA, they switched it up by wearing superhero costumes. They toured the city goofing around hilariously and looking for ways to combat evil. They even took their plastic dog Ketchup to a groomer and got the staff to give him a bath!

Ashton practices his sales technique in preparation for the great 5SOS pressing parties.

The 5SOS boys have always been our heroes; now they're *superheroes!*

Filming the awesome video for "Don't Stop." Hold on tight there, boys!

The boys are always willing to make a little harmless mayhem, and their Target store prank is now legend. They dressed up as store employees, complete with fake name tags and American accents, and attempted to sell their new album to passing customers. Ash announced, "We're going to be pretty much trying to sell our album to middle-aged men." The undercover band dropped CDs into random carts, sent customers looking for microwaves to the CD section, and attempted to push their album to unsuspecting shoppers. One customer even asked Luke if that was him on the CD cover. He denied it!

"WE'RE GOING TO BE PRETTY MUCH TRYING TO SELL OUR ALBUM TO MIDDLE-AGED MEN." Ashton

The producers of *Jimmy Kimmel Live!* asked some fans in the crowd to head backstage and record a video message for the group. They were amazed enough to be greeted by a member of 5SOS on screen, speaking straight to them. Asked to kiss their idol on the screen, they were tricked into puckering up for some wrinkly old man instead. Disappointed? Not when the real 5SOS stars appeared in person for a hug and a word of thanks!

Over the past couple of years, 5SOS have spent plenty of time on the road with the One Direction boys—certainly long enough to have some fun with the chart-topping boy band. After the two bands had performed together onstage in Manchester, at their final U.K. joint show, the 5SOS guys donned paper masks of One Direction and ambushed them onstage. They went one better in Melbourne. Luke tweeted a warning before the show— "Excited for the pranks tonight haha"—but no one expected a full-scale cream pie fight to break out as the two bands played together on the final song of the tour.

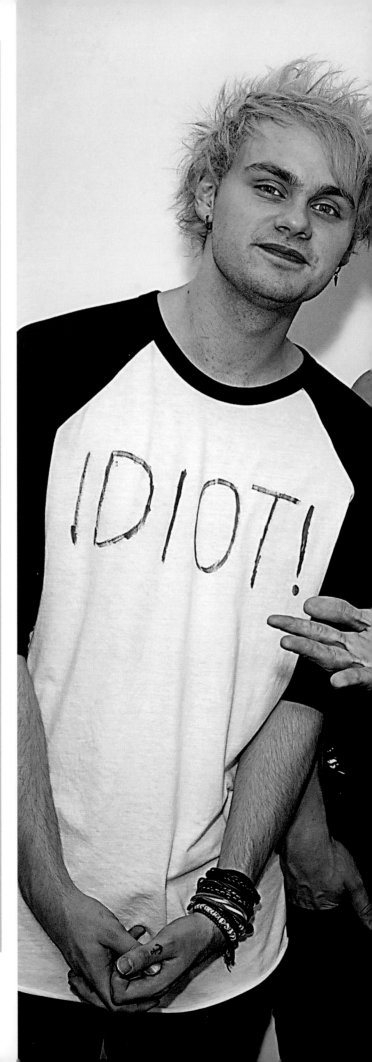

It may be a picture of innocence, but you can bet they're dreaming up some mischief!

43

"Tongues out on the count of three." Hang on! Luke and Mikey aren't ready!

5SOS IN EUROPE

WHEN 5SOS LEFT AUSTRALIA, THEIR FIRST STOP WAS
EUROPE—WHERE THOUSANDS OF FANS WERE ALREADY
WAITING FOR THEM.

5 Seconds of Summer
brought their magic
to Europe. And the
fans loved it.

The band enjoys the red carpet at the prestigious Brit Awards in London.

hen 5SOS first created a stir on YouTube, many of their most devoted fans lived thousands of miles away on the other side of the globe. It was only a matter of time before they met those fans face to face and showed them the energy and fun of a real punk-pop band. And yet, who would have guessed it would be a boy band, One Direction—five singers who have never lifted a guitar—who got them out of Australia and into the world? "It's incredible. We're on the other side of the world and it's a whole new thing for us, so it's been absolutely amazing to have that kind of support," said Ashton.

In 2012, 5SOS spent time in London and concentrated on their songwriting. They could see Wembley stadium from their apartment and dreamed of playing there. It's hard to believe, but within a year they did. The iconic venue became just one of the stadiums they rocked as they traveled across Britain, supporting One Direction on their tour, and picking up new fans with their power riffs, sweet harmonies, and instantly memorable choruses.

"IF IT'S GOT OUR FANS, IT'S GOING TO BE AWESOME. WE JUST WANT TO PUT ON A GOOD SHOW FOR THEM." Luke

Others in Europe would soon get their own taste of 5SOS up front and personal. The band embarked on a meet-and-greet acoustic tour, *Five Countries, Five Days*, which took place in Stockholm, Madrid, Berlin, Paris, and Milan. They really had no idea what to expect, but as Luke said, "If it's got our fans, it's going to be awesome. We just want to put on a good show for them." Calum added, "We don't overthink it. Hopefully the fans come with the energy. It's going to be wicked!"

The acoustic shows featured the four boys lined up at the front of the stage. It delivered new and old songs to the fans, and introduced the band to the kind of mayhem they could expect on the road. They were amazed by the reception they got in every new country. Fans chased their cars down the streets after concerts and surrounded their hotel until late at night. The boys loved it! "That Europe trip was quite mental," recalls Michael. "It got pretty intense, but we were there to make a ruckus anyway."

When 5SOS returned to European stages as the opening act on One Direction's *Where We Are Tour*, they had a best-selling album in nearly all the countries they visited. The excitement that greeted the release across the continent was as frenzied as anything in the U.S. or in their homeland. The guys were blown away by it all!

This time they played in massive stadiums in the U.K., Sweden, Denmark, France, Holland, Italy, Germany, Switzerland, Spain, and Portugal. It was daunting, but incredibly exciting. They made sure they held on to who they were and what made them special, while carefully watching how the 1D boys did it. "Learning how to tour from the lads really changed our lives," admits Calum.

The European leg of the tour was extraordinary. "The concert at the Stade de France was one of the best we've ever played," beams Michael. "It was loud and a good atmosphere." Ash agrees and adds, "French people realize that when you go to a concert you can just go crazy. It's really cool." Wherever the band went, their songs, stage presence, exuberance, and intense relationship with their fans won over new friends. Another continent had been conquered.

2015 will see them play to more than 240,000 fans across Europe in their biggest run of headline shows to date. "They still like our band, which is weird because we don't sing in other languages," says Ash. "They like our characters, even though they might not understand half of the things we do—and we love them for that."

"THAT EUROPE TRIP WAS QUITE MENTAL. IT GOT PRETTY INTENSE, BUT WE WERE THERE TO MAKE A RUCKUS ANYWAY." Michael

5SOS made more fans and friends across Europe with fantastic performances like this one in Milan, Italy.

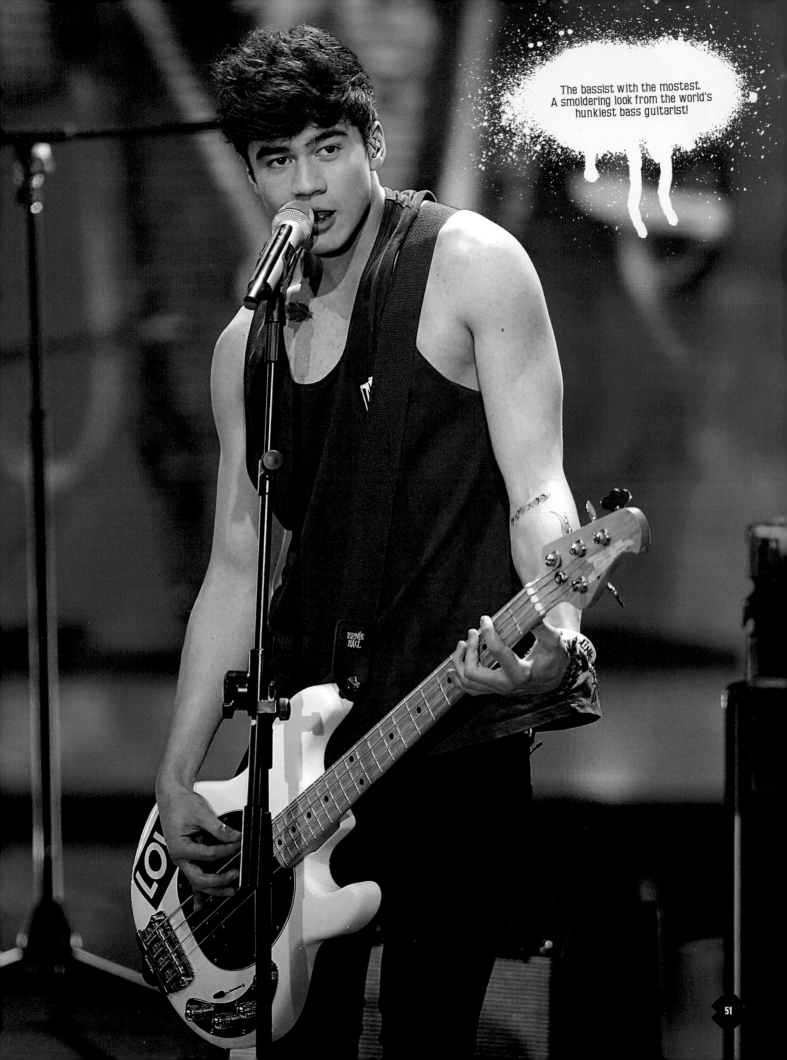

The bassist with the mostest. A smoldering look from the world's hunkiest bass guitarist!

"Expect loads of energy on stage...expect guitars... basically one big party," says Ashton. He's not kidding!

52

LIVE AND KICKING!

THE ENERGY AND EXHILARATION OF A 5SOS LIVE SHOW IS THE RESULT OF HARD WORK, THE BOYS' DESIRE TO ENTERTAIN, AND FANS WHO KNOW HOW TO GET A PARTY GOING.

"We feel quite comfortable on stage," says Luke. "That's our happy place."

"We feel quite comfortable on stage," says Luke. "That's our happy place." They certainly look happy and that's because these guys are born entertainers. They put their all into a performance and transmit their enthusiasm, sense of fun, and passion for the music to an already hyped-up crowd. The result is one noisy, sweaty, full-on party.

It almost seems wrong to call it a "performance" when so much of what they do is simply what comes naturally to four boys who just want to rock out. The amazing guitar and drum solos, the anthemic chants, and the sheer joy of belting out their favorite tunes haven't changed since they rehearsed in the garage in Sydney.

Even in those early days they knew they could be one of the greatest live bands around. "We were building a fan base, but we sort of wanted to be like a live band known for our live performances," says Ashton. "So that was the biggest job—transferring a YouTube audience to people who actually come down to our show."

So they worked and worked at being a great live act. "We did everything," Ash continues. "We rehearsed in the dark! We thought if we can't see what we're doing and we can still play, then we might sound good

"Altogether now: 'Hey, hey, hey, hey.'" The band's concert sing-a-long with fans are an integral part of a 5SOS performance.

"WE WERE BUILDING A FAN BASE, BUT WE SORT OF WANTED TO BE LIKE A LIVE BAND KNOWN FOR OUR LIVE PERFORMANCES." Ashton

Brothers in arms: Mikey and Luke hitting the groove.

Luke is intense and amazing at Shepherd's Bush Empire in London.

The same two boys who played on the school
stage together... now play sellout shows.

This is no boy band... these guys are serious about their music.

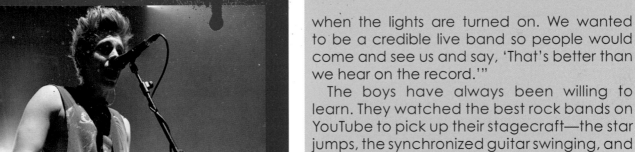

Luke takes up a classic rock guitarist pose. Well, he has the legs for it!

when the lights are turned on. We wanted to be a credible live band so people would come and see us and say, 'That's better than we hear on the record.'"

The boys have always been willing to learn. They watched the best rock bands on YouTube to pick up their stagecraft—the star jumps, the synchronized guitar swinging, and the way band members face the drummer to highlight his solos. When they finally got to meet their heroes in person they were eager to pick up pointers—when to share a microphone, how to spin guitars around their backs, and how to exit the chorus of a song gracefully.

There was one more element to their performance—their fans. 5SOS audiences are fanatical, and their passion, excitement, and ear-bursting screams create an exhilarating atmosphere. Playing in front of an audience that has already worked itself to fever pitch adds a new dimension to a performance. The group feeds off the passion of their fans and increases their energy levels even further, which makes the crowd even wilder. "It's a

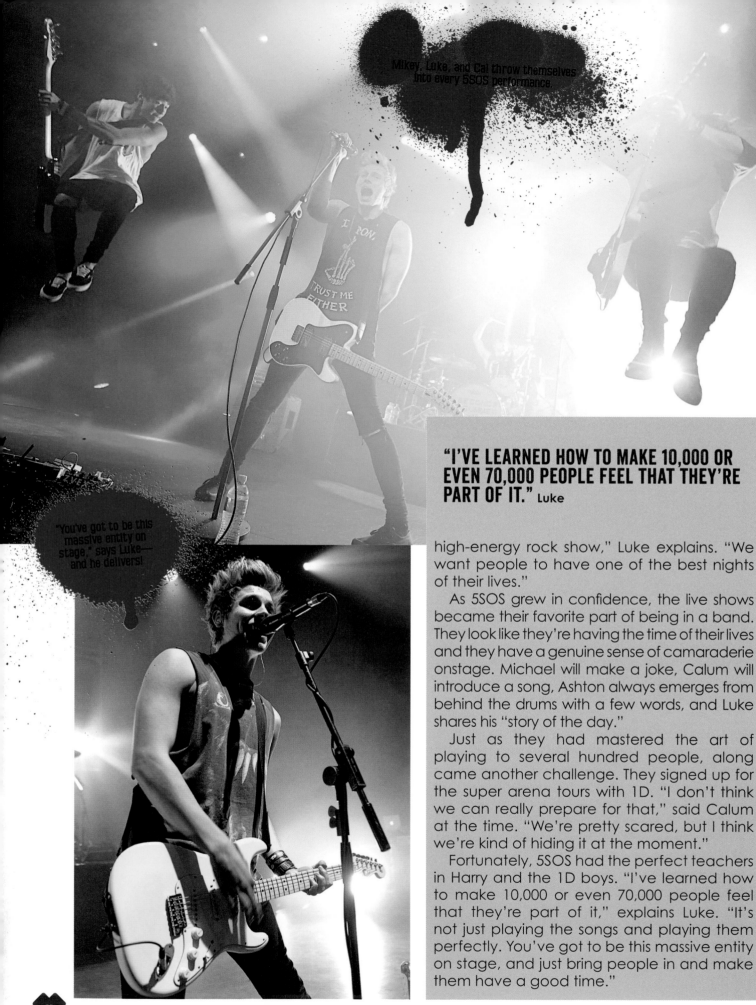

Mikey, Luke, and Cal throw themselves into every 5SOS performance.

"You've got to be this massive entity on stage," says Luke—and he delivers!

"I'VE LEARNED HOW TO MAKE 10,000 OR EVEN 70,000 PEOPLE FEEL THAT THEY'RE PART OF IT." Luke

high-energy rock show," Luke explains. "We want people to have one of the best nights of their lives."

As 5SOS grew in confidence, the live shows became their favorite part of being in a band. They look like they're having the time of their lives and they have a genuine sense of camaraderie onstage. Michael will make a joke, Calum will introduce a song, Ashton always emerges from behind the drums with a few words, and Luke shares his "story of the day."

Just as they had mastered the art of playing to several hundred people, along came another challenge. They signed up for the super arena tours with 1D. "I don't think we can really prepare for that," said Calum at the time. "We're pretty scared, but I think we're kind of hiding it at the moment."

Fortunately, 5SOS had the perfect teachers in Harry and the 1D boys. "I've learned how to make 10,000 or even 70,000 people feel that they're part of it," explains Luke. "It's not just playing the songs and playing them perfectly. You've got to be this massive entity on stage, and just bring people in and make them have a good time."

Luke hitting the right note at 5SOS's acclaimed show in Perth, Australia.

CALUM

HE COULD HAVE BEEN AUSTRALIA'S GREATEST SOCCER PLAYER. INSTEAD, HE SET HIS HEART ON BEING ITS GREATEST BASS PLAYER...

They call bass guitarist Calum Hood "the chilled-out one."

Calum has his own fans among the 5SOS faithful and he's always ready to acknowledge them.

Just a few years ago, it looked like Calum would follow a career in soccer. These days you're more likely to find Calum practicing his soccer skills in hotel rooms as he takes on his bandmates in their favorite FIFA video game. (They nearly rejected Ash from joining the group because he didn't play!) So what happened? 5SOS, that's what! He spent a month training in soccer-crazed Brazil just as 5SOS was taking off. Then he had to make a decision—ball or band? But, the excitement of their first gig sealed it for the 15-year-old.

At school, guitar player Calum used to jam with either of the sworn enemies, Michael or Luke—but never both together. However, when the enemies (Michael and Luke) became friends and formed the band, it was Calum who nearly missed out on being a part of it. Fortunately, he showed the quiet determination

Calum desperately hoping he doesn't re-enact *that* trouser-splitting incident.

"HE STARTED US ALL ON SONGWRITING AND WE WERE, LIKE, WOW!" Luke

Like the other band members, Calum loves to perform onstage and meet as many fans as possible after the performance.

Calum was the first member of the band to write his own songs

that has served them all so well and, as he says, somehow "wedged his way in"!

Calum is a pretty laid-back guy, but he knows what he wants. He came up with the breakthrough track "Gotta Get Out" when the rest of the band didn't even know he could write songs! Not only did he discover his own talent, but, as Luke explains, he also inspired the rest of the group. "He started us all on songwriting and we were, like, wow!" As 5SOS has developed, so have Calum's songwriting skills. "We live a pretty weird life," he says. "Every day we're always doing something different, so it really helps, seeing different things and experiencing different people's perspectives. We find inspiration everywhere."

Calum is building up a fine collection of tattoos. His first was on his collarbone and it reads, "MMXII." That's 2012 in Roman numerals, which is the year that 5SOS was formed. Others include a bird with "Mali-Koa" written beneath it. He explains, "It's my sister's name. She's my best friend and no one else gets me like she does. I go to her for everything." He also has a tattoo of his parents' initials, to remind him of them when he's far from home. "Family is everything," he insists.

Beenie hat: check! Bass guitar: check! Calum is ready to rock the place.

"EVERY DAY WE'RE ALWAYS DOING SOMETHING DIFFERENT, SO IT REALLY HELPS, SEEING DIFFERENT THINGS AND EXPERIENCING DIFFERENT PEOPLE'S PERSPECTIVES. WE FIND INSPIRATION EVERYWHERE." Calum

"I'm still just a teenage kid learning from mistakes :)" he tweeted in 2014. Life on the road has certainly produced some embarrassing moments for the young bassist.

An inappropriate photo ended up all over the Internet when he famously split his trousers in front of 15,000 people during One Direction's *Take Me Home Tour* in LA. A roadie had to use duct tape to put them back together!

As the only dark-haired member of the band, Calum has his fair share of female admirers, but what kind of girl does the carefree boy from Sydney go for? "I'm quite weird, so I'd have to look for a quirky girl," he says. "I really like short hair, a sporty girl, anything—if a girl likes me, then I'll like her!"

BEST FANS FOREVER

AS THE GUYS ALWAYS SAY, THE MILLION-STRONG 5SOS "FAMILY" HAVE PUT THE BAND WHERE THEY ARE TODAY—ON TOP OF THE WORLD.

What a prize! Super-hunk Aston gives out one of his drumsticks to a very, very, very lucky 5SOS fan.

Every fan wants a picture of themselves with the band and the boys do their best to oblige.

A sh, Calum, Luke, and Michael have to pinch themselves to make sure it's really happening. Day after day they encounter the most devoted and amazing fans in the world—and there are literally millions of them. The guys certainly don't take their fans for granted, because they still remember all too clearly when they were playing to a dozen or so people in a seedy bar. "The fans own us," says Luke. "All the stuff we've achieved through our career is because of them. It's like the fans are doing the work behind the scenes."

Whichever way you want to count their fans, their numbers are astonishing. The band

has nearly three million followers on Instagram and five million on Twitter—and that's not including the guys' personal accounts. No band has ever used social media like 5SOS does. They want to make sure their fans know they are appreciated. They detail everything that happens in their lives (even what they're having for breakfast!), retweet their fans' posts, and express their big love for them all.

The band tries to follow any of the fans who follow them on social media, but what they love best is being able to meet them in person. In fact, they go out of their way to make themselves available for pictures, hugs, and a few words with as many fans as they

5SOS fans are without doubt the loudest and most devoted in the world, and the boys credit them with putting the band where it is.

"THE FANS OWN US. ALL THE STUFF WE'VE ACHIEVED THROUGH OUR CAREER IS BECAUSE OF THEM. IT'S LIKE THE FANS ARE DOING THE WORK BEHIND THE SCENES." Luke

The guys' signing sessions give them a chance to meet their fabulous fans.

Wherever the boys go in the world, they find adoring, enthusiastic, and crazy fans.

"Thanks, Luke—I Love You!" Another fan gets a priceless selfie.

can. They have set up impromptu acoustic concerts in city parks just hours before a concert and, in one amazing stunt, they even worked in the box office selling tickets to their own show!

In turn, the 5SOS "family," as the fans call themselves, take pretty good care of their idols. They send pizza to the boys' hotel room and shower them with gifts. "Our fans give us koala bear toys to remind us of home," says Ash. "They know what we need." Sometimes, though, they can be a little strange. In LA, two male strippers dressed as policemen were sent to serenade the boys, who insist that the odd moment doesn't stop them loving all their fans.

Even at the massive stadium concerts when 5SOS open for 1D, the boys are able to recognize their fans. "You can tell which ones are ours. They dress like us," says Calum. "They'll wear bandanas and they'll wear flannel shirts tied round their waist and they'll have like different colored hair, so it's pretty cool."

"REAL BANDS SAVE FANS; REAL FANS SAVE BANDS" HAS BECOME A MOTTO FOR THE 5SOS FAMILY." Michael

5SOS fans packed out Rockefeller Plaza when the band played there for *The TODAY Show*.

Mikey prides himself on being the best in the band at making faces for fans' selfies.

At the live shows the relationship between the band and their fanatical supporters creates a unique attitude. Michael's tweet "Real bands save fans; real fans save bands" has become a motto for the 5SOS family. There are banners with those words at every concert, alongside hundreds of others, professing love for the group. These are real fans: they make lots of noise, dance themselves crazy, and sing along to every song. "It was a dream of ours to be up on a stage playing our own original music and to have crowds sing our songs back at us!" reveals Ash. "At our first show in Sydney that happened and it was the most amazing thing ever."

Around the world, fans have been getting together to swap their 5SOS stories and to

"IT WAS A DREAM OF OURS TO BE UP ON A STAGE PLAYING OUR OWN ORIGINAL MUSIC AND TO HAVE CROWDS SING OUR SONGS BACK AT US!" Ashton

watch and listen to the band on screen. Imagine how frustrated the boys felt that they couldn't attend. So, in November 2014 they hosted their own super-fan convention. They called it Derp-Com and it gave lucky fans a chance to "fight ninjas, Internet haters, and join in some serious banding." Of course, it also gave the guys an opportunity to meet their favorite people—their fans.

The boys are dressed for fun at a signing session in California where fans hope to meet the boys face to face.

5SOS IN AUSTRALIA

HOME IS WHERE THE HEART IS, AND FOR THE 5SOS BOYS IT WILL ALWAYS BE WITH THEIR FAMILY, FANS, AND FRIENDS DOWN UNDER.

The boys are back in town: 5SOS's triumphant homecoming at the Enmore Theatre, Sydney.

"Remember us?" Luke serenades the Melbourne faithful in May 2014.

5 Seconds of Summer are from Australia—and they're proud of it! They're as Australian as kangaroos, koalas, and BBQs on the beach. Many rock bands demand that caviar and champagne are delivered to their dressing rooms after a show, but no matter where they are in the world these boys just ask for a supply of Vegemite—the classic Australian sandwich spread.

When they finish a tour and board the plane home, you can feel the excitement in their messages, even if the first thing Calum's mom usually says to him is: "Get a haircut!" It's not long before they're chilling out at home with their friends and family and their precious dogs, and they sink back easily into being everyday Aussie boys. "Michael and I are planning an end of summer BBQ," Ash told *We Love Pop* magazine in the fall of 2014. "We do this thing where we put a sprinkler under a trampoline, then jump in the sprinkler,

so it's like a water park in your garden. It's very Australian!"

In their early days, 5SOS worked hard to escape the Western Sydney suburbs. They never really felt appreciated there, and for a while it seemed like they had more fans outside Australia than in their own country. Things changed when they got their first break, opening for the U.S. band Hot Chelle Rae on its Australian tour. Suddenly the locals got them. A few more dates followed, but London—and 1D—were calling, so it would be a while before Australians saw them again.

When the band finally did come back, it

"WE'RE JUST FOUR REALLY WEIRD DUDES FROM WESTERN SYDNEY." 5SOS

Luke and Calum demonstrate the chemistry that makes 5SOS special.

In Australia, the band sets out to prove to their parents just why they have conquered the world.

Flying high! The guys treat the Perth crowd to an awesome high-octane show.

was to some incredible news: "She Looks So Perfect" had gone to No. 1 in Australia and New Zealand. "I actually cried of happiness today when I found out," tweeted Ashton. The short *Pants Down Tour* sold out in a matter of minutes and Luke said he felt real pride when his father told him that he had heard 5SOS singles being played in malls and stores in their local neighborhood.

When they returned home again with One Direction for the *Take Me Home Tour* in September 2013, they were mobbed at the airport. In an interview with the *West Australia* newspaper, Michael said, "It's incredible that every time we come back it's getting bigger and there's more support... It's crazy that people where we come from actually like the music we release!"

The *There's No Place Like Home Tour* saw them headlining their own major shows. They played in front of rapturous audiences across the country—in Sydney, Adelaide, Melbourne, Brisbane, and Perth. At their triumphant hometown show they announced themselves by saying, "We're just four really

"IT'S INCREDIBLE THAT EVERY TIME WE COME BACK IT'S GETTING BIGGER AND THERE'S MORE SUPPORT..." Michael

weird dudes from Western Sydney." They went on to rock the packed Enmore Theatre, with Calum telling fans, "Our families are here tonight, so we have to prove to them why we dropped out of school."

5SOS fever gripped Australia. In October 2014, the band played "Good Girls" and "Amnesia" on *The X Factor Australia*, and both the crowd and the judges gave the quartet a standing ovation at the end of their set. Then, as 2014 drew to a close, they were chosen to open the star-studded presentation ceremony of the Australian Record Industry Association (ARIA) Awards.

They might be global stars, but Michael, Luke, Ashton, and Calum have not forgotten where they came from. Australia loves to see their favorite sons returning and, as Luke points out, "Coming home is what helps keep us sane."

PROFILE
MICHAEL

WITH HIS EVER-CHANGING HAIR COLOR, EYE PIERCING, AND ALL-ACTION GUITAR STYLE, MICHAEL IS THE PUMPING HEART OF THE BAND.

Michael Clifford: one crazy, punked-up, fun-filled dude.

Watching 5SOS's guitar hero performing on stage or chatting easily with his 90s punk heroes, it's hard to imagine he used to be a geek who hated leaving his computer keyboard. Technology saved Michael in the form of the *Guitar Hero* game. Becoming an ace on the color-fretted console inspired his love of punk rock and made him believe that he could handle a real guitar.

And could he! Michael was given his first electric guitar when he was 11, and he practiced and practiced, playing along to tracks from his beloved Green Day and Blink 182. From there it was an obvious step to forming a group. At last, there was a point in going to school! "I don't think we had any expectations. We were just 'Let's make a band, have fun,'" he recalls. "All I really ever wanted was to be in a band. I think it was the same for all of us. We wouldn't be good at anything else."

"ALL I REALLY EVER WANTED WAS TO BE IN A BAND. I THINK IT WAS THE SAME FOR ALL OF US. WE WOULDN'T BE GOOD AT ANYTHING ELSE." Michael

As 5SOS began to edge their way to global domination, Michael began to create his own style. He dyed his fair hair in a "reverse skunk"—a bleach-blond mop with a stripe of black down the center. He soon got bored of that look, though, and dyed it again... and again... and again. He has changed his hair color more than twenty times—the orange, green, and electric blue were especially memorable—and he isn't going to stop anytime soon. He said recently, "I'm just going through the color wheel and checking out what I haven't done. Now I'm going to have to start to do patterns!"

Mikey at the mike. When it comes to music, he does get serious.

A fan's collection wouldn't be complete without a tongues-out pic with Mikey!

After gigs, Michael doesn't trash hotel rooms like rock stars are known to do. "What's the point of throwing a TV out the window if SpongeBob SquarePants could be on?" Instead he releases his inner geek. He's a video game fanatic and spends hours playing *League of Legends*. Like the rest of the band, he also spends a lot of time on Twitter, where his profile reads: "If you like me, I probably like you more. I play in a band, so do other people in my band."

"IF YOU LIKE ME, I PROBABLY LIKE YOU MORE. I PLAY IN A BAND, SO DO OTHER PEOPLE IN MY BAND." Michael

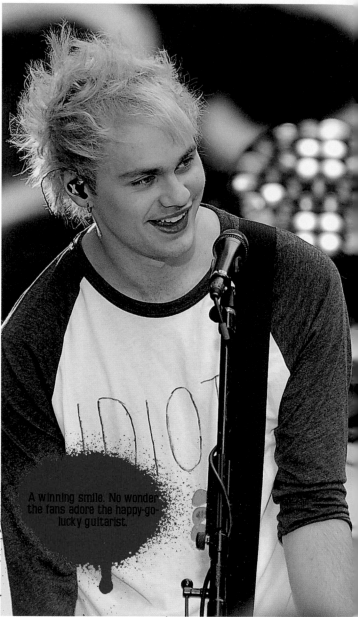

A winning smile. No wonder the fans adore the happy-go-lucky guitarist.

On stage and off, Michael savors every moment of his time on tour with the band.

Although he is currently single, rumor—or rather, Luke's big mouth—has it that Michael is on the lookout for a girlfriend. "My dream girl would be funny, weird, and caring!" he has declared. "I don't know if I've met her yet, but then again, maybe I have and just haven't known it." He also admits that catching the eye of a good-looking girl in the 5SOS crowd sometimes distracts him so much that he forgets the words to a song!

The guitarist is still pleasantly surprised by the attention he receives from girls wherever the band travels around the world. "It's so weird to us that girls actually like us," he told *The Australian*, "because when we were growing up I was so clingy—I was like 'Please date me! Please like me!'" Then, with his beguiling smile he added, "I'm still like that!"

Michael on stage in Las Vegas—just trying to take it all in.

TOTAL EXPOSURE

WITH EVERY AWARD CEREMONY, MUSIC VIDEO SHOW, AND TV SHOW THEY PERFORM ON, 5SOS WIN OVER MILLIONS MORE FANS.

5SOS performs live during the 2014 MTV Video Music Awards.

Another landmark date in the short but intense history of 5 Seconds of Summer was May 18, 2014. It was the day they appeared at the *Billboard Music Awards in Las Vegas.* From then on, the "secret" of 5SOS was out. They were the talk of the town, the country, the world. The band took to the red carpet like old pros, unfazed by Kendall Jenner almost introducing them as One Direction, and "She Looks So Perfect" stole the show. Even Beyoncé was moved to tweet, "*5 Seconds of Summer* are about to take *America* by storm!"

Within months, 5SOS picked up their first major award. They won a cherished Moonman for best lyric video at the MTV Video Music Awards. Michael made it clear how much it meant to the band. "Cannot believe we've just won a VMA," he tweeted. "All of this is thanks to you guys. Best fans EVURRRRRRRR. I love you."

The music video was another great opportunity for the band to express their personalities. For "Don't Stop" they took the

"5 SECONDS OF SUMMER ARE ABOUT TO TAKE AMERICA BY STORM!" Beyoncé

The boys have quickly gotten used to treading the red carpet at awards ceremonies.

Who are these guys again? The 5SOS interview before the *Billboard* Music Awards.

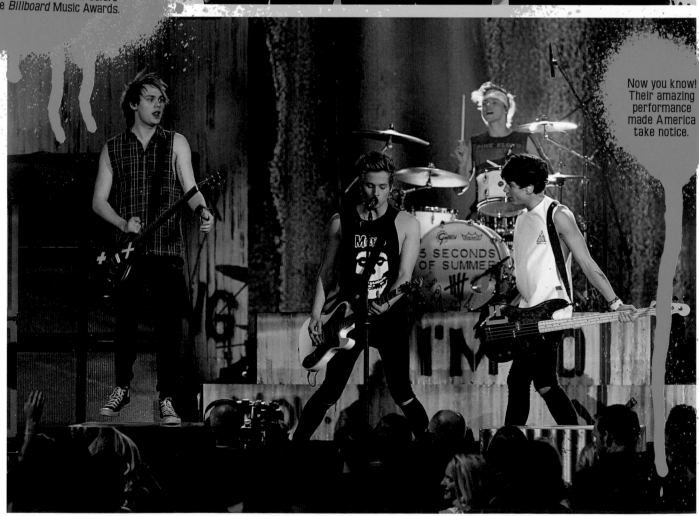

Now you know! Their amazing performance made America take notice.

"THANK YOU FOR MAKING THE TODAY SHOW AWESOME, THE 5SOS FANS LITERALLY TOOK OVER THE CITY." Ashton

role of fun superhero characters fighting ninjas and evil—Luke was Dr Fluke, Michael was Mike-Ro-Wave, Ashton was Smash, and Calum was Cal Pal. It was director Isaac Rentz's idea. "The second I saw how charismatic and fun-loving the boys were, I thought I gotta use this idea for this band right here!" he said.

Their other videos are just as crazy. In "She Looks So Perfect," their song has the effect of making people—of all shapes and appearances—take their clothes off. "We've never wanted anything more than for people to get nude in a video of ours," claimed a grinning Ashton. Then, the "Good Girls" video saw the boys taking over a girls' school and causing real chaos.

Meanwhile, 5SOS was causing a stir on national TV in America. Fans camped out for days before the band rocked out the Rockefeller Plaza on their appearance on *The TODAY Show*. The crowds were the biggest the show had ever seen, leading

Luke to tweet, "Thank you for making the today show awesome, the 5SOS fans literally took over the city." On *Jimmy Kimmel Live!* they pulled the best-ever kissing prank on some astonished devotees, and on *Good Morning America* they performed some kicking acoustic performances of "Amnesia" and "She Looks So Perfect."

On *The Tonight Show* with Jimmy Fallon, the boys showed what great sports they are by playing along with his Hashtags game. They had to play hit songs with the words changed by viewers to reflect the fall season. They rose to the challenge brilliantly. Calum apologized to Jay-Z before a Halloween version of "99 Problems" and a tweet about hot wings, football, and raking leaves was sung to Blink 182's "All The Small Things." They even laughed at themselves, Michael breaking into fits of giggles before finishing his lyric, "He looks so perfect hanging there, in his flannel shirt and long straw hair. Now I know, it's a scarecrow!"

So proud! The boys show off their first Moonman after the 2014 MTV Awards.

CREDITS

The publishers would like to thank the following sources for their kind permission to reproduce the pictures in this book.

Key: t=Top, b=Bottom, c=Center, l=Left and r=Right.

2 Cindy Ord/Getty Images; 4 Stefania D'Alessandro/ Getty Images; 5 Stefania D'Alessandro/Getty Images; 6t Larry Busacca/Billboard/Getty Images; 6b Lester Cohen/Getty Images; 8 Charles Sykes/Invision/Press Association Images; 9 Norwest Christian College; 10 MediaPunch/Rex Features; 11 Norwest Christian College; 12 James McCauley/Rex Features; 13 Paul A. Hebert/Invision/Press Association Images; 14 Henning Kaiser/DPA/Press Association Images; 15t Jerome Domine/ABACA/Press Association Images; 15b Yui Mok/PA Wire/Press Association Images; 16 Jason Kemplin/Getty Images; 17t Mark Metcalfe/Getty Images; 17b Kevin Winter/Billboard/Getty Images; 18 Larry Marano/Getty Images; 19 Myrna Suarez/Getty Images; 20 Stefania D'Alessandro/Getty Images; 21t C Brandon/Getty Images; 21b Jeff Kravitz/MTV1415/ Getty Images; 22-23 Kevin Mazur/OneD/Getty Images; 24 Myrna Suarez/Getty Images; 25t Kevin Winter/Billboard/Getty Images; 25b PictureGroup/Rex Features; 26 Larry Busacca/Billboard/Getty Images; 27 Chris Pizzello/AP/Press Association Images; 28t Jeff Kravitz/MTV1415/Getty Images; 28b Erik Pendzich/Rex Features; 29 Chris Pizzello/AP/Press Association Images; 30 Shirlaine Forrest/Getty Images; 31 Matt Baron/BEI/ Rex Features; 32t Ashton Irwin/Getty Images; 32b Larry Marano/Getty Images; 33 Kevin Mazur/Getty Images; 34 Chance Yeh/Getty Images; 35 Isaac Brekken/ Getty Images; 36 Jason Kempin/Getty Images; 37t Frazer Harrison/Getty Images; 37b Steve Meddle/ ITV/Rex Features; 38 Ray Tamarra/Getty Images; 39 Shirlaine Forrest/Getty Images; 40 Suzan/Empics Entertainment/Press Association Images; 41t Suzan/ EMPICS Entertainment/Press Association Images; 41b Suzan/EMPICS Entertainment/Press Association Images; 42-43 Suzan/Empics Entertainment/Press Association Images; 44-45 Christopher Polk/Getty Images; 46 Andrew Benge/Getty Images; 47 David M. Benett/Getty Images; 48-49 Marco Bertorello/Getty Images; 50 Stefania D'Alessandro/Getty Images; 51 Stefania D'Alessandro/Getty Images; 52-53 Andrew Benge/Getty Images; 54-55 Mark Metcalfe/Getty Images; 56 Andrew Benge/Getty Images; 57t Andrew Benge/Getty Images; 57b C Brandon/Getty Images; 58 Jo Hale/Getty Images; 59t Jo Hale/Getty Images; 59b C Brandon/Getty Images; 60t Matt Jelonek/ Getty Images; 60b C Brandon/Getty Images; 61 Matt Jelonek/Getty Images; 62 Shirlaine Forrest/Getty Images; 63t Christopher Polk/Billboard/Getty Images; 63b Matt Jelonek/Getty Images; 64-65 Jeff Kravitz/ Getty Images; 66 Jeff Kravitz/Getty Images; 67 Kevin Winter/MTV1415/Getty Images; 68-69 Stephen Lovekin/ Getty Images; 70 Larry Marano/Getty Images; 71t Graham Denholm/Getty Images; 71b Suzan/Empics Entertainment/Press Association Images; 72 Graham Denholm/Getty Images; 73 Beretta/Sims/Rex Features; 74t Chance Yeh/Getty Images; 74b Larry Marano/ Getty Images; 75 Paul A. Hebert/AP/Press Association Images; 76-77 Mark Metcalfe/Getty Images; 78 Graham Denholm/Getty Images; 79 Scott Legato/ Getty Images; 80-81 Scott Legato/Getty Images; 82 Matt Jelonek/Getty Images; 83t Graham Denholm/ Getty Images; 83b Mark Metcalfe/Getty Images; 84 Shirlaine Forrest/Getty Images; 85 Kevin Mazur/ OneD/Getty Images; 86 Stefania D'Alessandro/Getty Images; 87 Beretta/Sims/Rex Features; 88l Christopher Polk/Billboard/Getty Images; 88r Chance Yeh/Getty Images; 89 Michael Tran/Getty Images; 90 Jeff Kravitz/ MTV1415/Getty Images; 91 Anthony Harvey/Getty Images; 92t Jeffrey Mayer/Getty Images; 92b Ethan Miller/Getty Images; 93 Kevin Mazur/Getty Images; 94-95 Kevin Winter/Billboard/Getty Images.

Every effort has been made to acknowledge correctly and contact the source and/or copyright holder of each picture and Carlton Books Limited apologizes for any unintentional errors or omissions, which will be corrected in future editions of this book.

First published in 2015 by
Carlton Books
20 Mortimer Street
London W1T 3JW

10 9 8 7 6 5 4 3 2

Text copyright © Carlton Books Limited 2015
Design copyright © Carlton Books Limited 2015

A CIP catalogue record for this book is available from the British Library.

ISBN: 978-1-78312-125-0

Design: Adam Wright
Project Art Editor: James Pople
Editorial: Caroline Curtis
Picture Research: Emma Copestake
Production: Rachel Burgess
Senior Project Editor: Matt Lowing

Printed in Dubai, UAE